STEM CELL BANKING AND ITS PROSPECTIVE

PHOOL CHANDRA | NEETU SACHAN | RAJNI MALHOTRA

Dedicated to my beloved parents

Mrs. Ram Devi and Shri Ganga Vishnu

Contents

Preface

The authors feel great pleasure in presenting the First Edition of the book Stem Cell Banking and its Prospectives .

The subject matter has been discussed in such a simple way that the readers will find no difficulty to understand. Every effort has been made to explain the subject matter in such a simple way that the readers can easily understand. We have tried our best to keep the book free from misprints. The authors shall be grateful to the readers who point out errors and omissions which, inspite of all care, might have been there.

The authors in general hope that the present book will be warmly received by the sreaders. We shall indeed be very thankful to our colleagues for their recommending this book to their students.

The authors wish to express their thanks to the Notion Publishers for bringing out this book in the present nice form.

The authors will feel amply rewarded if the book serves the purpose for which it is meant. The suggestions for the improvement of the book are always welcome and will be highly appreciated.

- The Authors

Acknowledgements

We have the privilege of meeting people who affect our lives in such a way that they are never the same again as we continue down the path of life. They made our lives worth living by simple considerate acts such as a smile, a helping hand, a word of encouragement, or simply by being present.

Research is a collaborative effort. It is the result of various butaneous personalities' efforts. It's never easy to put into words how grateful we are for the wonderful brains that have accompanied us on this path of completing as a project. At this point, it brings us great pleasure to express our gratitude to all of the beautiful people who have guided and enriched us with their unwavering ideals.

To begin, we bow in reverence to almighty God for giving us the patience, zeal, and strength to complete this project effectively.

Our heartfelt gratitude to the honorable Vice-Chancellor, **Prof. (Dr.) M.P. Pandey**, for providing the necessary infrastructure and facilities throughout this work.

Dr. Navneet Verma, Dean, Faculty of Pharmacy, IFTM University Moradabad, and **Dr. Sushil Kumar**, Director, School of Pharmaceutical Sciences, IFTM University, have our heartfelt gratitude and sincere thanks for their continual encouragement and support throughout the project.

Words are inadequate to express my heartfelt gratitude and deep appreciation to our family members for their unwavering support, blessings, affection, kind collaboration, loving companionship, and moral support. It gives us great pleasure to express our gratitude to loving **Siddhi** and **Avi**, whose affection and constant care provided us with emotional support and the motivation to work hard toward our objective.

CHAPTER ONE

Introduction

The mother is the panacea for all kinds of calamities. The act of giving birth is the only movement when both pain and pleasure converge in a moment of time. It is in the manner of the sharp point of a needle, astride upon that points are both pleasure and pain, simultaneously assailing the female that is undergoing the miracle of childbirth[1]. The maternal bond between a human female and her biological child usually begins to develop during pregnancy. A critical link that supports and nourishes the baby in the womb for 9 months is the umbilical cord[2]. It is called a lifeline and it is through this cord that the placenta and the fetus are attached to each other[3].Twenty years have passed since the first report of a successful cord blood transplant was reported in 1989 in a child with Fanconi's anemia. During these 20 years, the cord blood field has had dramatic growth, with over 400,000 cord blood units donated and stored worldwide for unrelated use [4]. An average of 120 mL of blood can be collected with no risk to either the mother or the baby [5]. The cord blood is then processed, where Stem cells are isolated and stored in the vapor phase of liquid nitrogen for future use Cord blood is currently used to treat approximately 70 diseases including leukemias, lymphomas, anemias, and Severe Combined Immunodeficiency (SCID)[6]. Cord blood contains all the normal elements of blood which are red blood cells, white blood cells, platelets, and plasma. It is also, rich in multi-potent hematopoietic stem cells (HSCs), similar to those found in bone marrow[7]. In the human body, there are three main sources of stem cells: embryonic, adult (or mature), and umbilical cells[8,9]. Stem cells from different sources have been used mainly for research purposes. Potential medical applications of stem cells include inflammatory, neurodegenerative, musculoskeletal, and metabolic diseases and diseases of the heart and blood vessels[10,11]. Hematopoietic stem cells (HSCs) derived from bone marrow were the first adult stem cells used for therapy[11]. Cryopreservation is one of the techniques for cell preservation that involves the following steps: a) pre-freeze processing; b) introduction of a cryopreservation solution; c) freezing protocol; d) storage conditions; e) thawing conditions and f) post-thaw assessment. Hematopoietic Stem Cells preservation focused mainly on modification of the freezing medium and freezing and storage protocols. Dimethyl sulfoxide is used to cryopreserve HSCs, with a DMSO concentration of 10% being the most commonly used[12],[13]. The possibility of re-creating in the laboratory a pluripotent state in stromal fibroblastic cells and other differentiated somatic cell types [e.g. induced pluripotent stem (iPS) cells] introduces the idea of personalized stem cell therapy and may lead to the development of substances for regenerative medicine [14],[15].

At birth, the umbilical cord CB was first recognized as a rich source of hematopoietic stem and progenitor cells (HSCs) several decades ago extends between 30-65cm in length has a mean diameter of 1.5 cm, and weights 40 grams[17]. Umbilical cord blood (CB) is firmly established as an unrelated donor source for hematopoietic stem cell transplantation (HSCT) and is a readily available cell source in the evolving fields of regenerative medicine and cellular therapies. Worldwide, there are over 160 public banks with a global inventory of over 700,000 fully characterized, high-quality cord blood units (CBUs)[18], and more than 5 million CBUs have been banked at an estimated 215 family banks. In this chapter, we review the history of CB transplantation (CBT) and banking as well as established and emerging clinical uses of CB in regenerative medicine. CB was first recognized as a rich source of hematopoietic stem and progenitor cells (HSCs) several decades ago[19]. Building on this initial success, additional related donor CBTs were performed in selected centers over the next 5 years; the first unrelated donor CB bank was established by Dr. Pablo Rubinstein at the New York Blood Center in 1992. In the following year, Dr. Joanne Kurtzberg performed the first unrelated donor CBT at Duke University in a 4-year-old child with relapsed T-cell leukemia. Early experience with unrelated CBT demonstrated that partially HLA-mismatched, banked unrelated donor CB could successfully restore hematopoiesis with an incidence of graft versus host disease (GvHD) lower than expected and that engraftment was associated with the total nucleated cell (TNC) dose available relative to the recipient's body size[20],[21].

A technique of cord blood stem cell transplant which may eventually remove the need for matched bone marrow transplants has been used in humans for the first time. It is hoped that "master cells" taken from umbilical cords could be used on any patient without rejection. The latest advance, published in the journal nature medicine, greatly multiplies the tiny number of cells from the cord ready for a transplant [22].

Studies have shown that siblings have up to 75% chances of compatibility, and the cord blood may even be a match for parents and grandparents up to 50%. In 1995 a total of 320 centers worldwide had more than 66,000 transplants [23]. Stem cells characterized by the potential of self-renewal and differentiation have so far shown promising results in the treatment of both malignant and non-malignant disorders. The umbilical cord connects the fetus to the placenta and mediates the supply of oxygen and nutrients to the developing fetus. In the human body, there are three main sources of stem cells: embryonic, adult (or mature), and umbilical cells. It is approximately 50-70 cm long and 2 cm in diameter, is known to mediate the fetoplacental circulation and has its origin from the same zygote which gives rise to the foetus[24]. Cord blood cells isolated from the clamped umbilical cord differ from those of bone marrow and peripheral blood in composition, number as well as properties. Cord blood is a rich source of hematopoietic stem cells[25].

CHAPTER TWO

Stem Cell Banking Approaches

Cord Blood

Most CB banks have adopted the use of small (i.e., paediatric) blood bags (approximately 250 cc in size); although collections can also be made with 60 cc syringes. Bag collections are preferred as collection of the blood (and subsequent processing) occurs in a closed system (preferable for most regulatory stipulations). However, bag collections must not be left unattended in order to prevent unintended contamination or loss of blood flow from occurring. Routinely, collections are completed within 5 min (prior to placental expulsion after clamping and sectioning of the cord) by accessing the umbilical vein. Alternatively, one can wait for delivery of the placenta and collect the blood directly from the expelled placenta. The vast majority of the cellular constituent in the cord blood collection is red blood cells (RBC), followed by neutrophils (making up 70%–80% of the leukocyte population). In reality only the mononuclear (MNC) fraction (20% of the leukocyte population), which contains the stem cell population, is needed for banking. The stem cells make up approximately 1% of the MNC fraction. CB has a very high hematocrit and RBC can make up more than half of the collection by volume. Thus, to facilitate the banking procedure, the vast majority of CB collections are RBC-depleted or reduced prior to cryopreservation. Several methods are in use to accomplish this goal including; He span sedimentation to obtain a modified buffy coat[26]. There are a few CB banks that perform plasma reduction as a means of volume reduction prior to banking. It is thought that there may be important components in the non-leukocyte fraction that would be important for clinical use[27].

Cord Tissue

Source of stem cells that can be simultaneously obtained at birth is the cord tissue (CT) itself which is a ready source of MSCs. CT can be collected and banked as a future source of stem cells for regenerative medicine and tissue engineering. In addition to MSCs, CT also contains endothelial and epithelial precursor cells that may be useful for these applications Theoretically, MSCs could be isolated either from cord blood or from cord tissue [27,28]. Specific optimal parameters needed to be met in order to obtain significant numbers of blood-derived MSCs; including CB collections larger than 90 cc and processing of such samples within 2 h of birth. Even when these restrictions were met the absolute numbers of MSCs isolated from CB were too low for immediate use (in the hundreds to thousands of cells); although the MSCs could be rapidly expanded in vitro to 1×10^9 MSC in several weeks to several months. Thus, in reality, CT is really the only clinically feasible source of MSCs at the time of birth [29,30]. CT is derived from the human umbilical cord that develops during gestation to support the development of the foetus. The average length of the cord itself is between 30 and 50 cm depending on a variety of factors including maternal age, heath and ethnicity[31]. Stem cells have been identified in various anatomical locations throughout the cord tissue including the amniotic compartment, the Wharton's jelly and the perivascular space surrounding the blood vessels[32]. If it is assumed that the average length of CT that could be readily obtained at birth will 30 cm [33], the number of freshly isolated MSC would range from 750,000 to 150×10^6 cells assuming every cell isolated would actually an MSC [34].

Adipose Tissue

All adipose samples can be obtaining with written consent from the donors and according to any other requirements of the local Institution Review Board (IRB). Adipose tissue samples are generally obtained from scheduled liposuction procedures, or by syringe harvest performed under local anaesthesia. The lipo aspirates should be process and cryopreserve within 24–36 h of collection. For cryopreservation, wash the tissue extensively with isotonic saline, and the wash tissue slurry place directly in a cryo-container (generally a cryobag) and add an equal volume of pre-cooled dimethyl sulfoxide (DMSO) solution (70% Lactated Ringer's buffer, 20% serum or HSA, 20% DMSO) slowly over several minutes at 4 °C. The cryo-container is generally mix at 4 °C for 20–30 min to allow for cryoprotectant equilibration. Cryopreservation is perform using a control rate freezer to –180 °C before final submersion in liquid nitrogen for long term storage[35].

CHAPTER THREE

Basic Principles of Cell Banking

Stem cell banking for therapeutic use requires several standards to be maintained:

Quality

Development of processing methods to generate cells in compliance with current good manufacturing practices (GMP) to ensure the quality of the products. Commission Directive 2003/94/EC of October 2003 regulates the principles and guidelines of GMP with respect to medicinal products for human use and investigational products in Europe.

Safety

Applying strict measures to avoid the risk of disease transmission. Cellular therapy products are derived from human sources and, therefore, carry the risk of transmitting infectious agents.

Efficiency

Providing products that maintain the biological properties that are useful for human health (clinical perspective) and performing all the activities related to stem cell banking at a lower cost without reducing the quality.

Traceability

Allowing the ability to track specific information at every step in the process chain. This must be achieved confidentially.

Transparency

Offering accurate information to users and institutional organisms according to current concepts in medicine and regulations.

Benchmarking

Establishing indicators to compare the model with other ones and optimizing the services by implementing a continuing program of Quality Improvement. Basic principles of GMP guidelines involve quality assurance, personnel, premises and equipment, documentation, production, quality control, complaints and product recalls, and self-inspection and quality audits [36]. Centralization is especially important for public non-profit banks. The international network of umbilical cord blood banks, intended to achieve the fast and efficient location of products according to human leukocyte antigen (HLA) compatibility criteria, is a good example of the implementation of common standards for international cooperation in stem cell banking [37].

CHAPTER FOUR

Donation and Collection

Donation

Cells and tissues are usually collected under operating theatre conditions. An aseptic environment is fundamental to minimizing the risk of contamination. In either case, specific environmental conditions (container, temperature, transport solution, etc.) must be established to maintain cell viability and function according to cell bank requirements [40]. Umbilical cord blood is usually collected in a bag containing approximately 23 ml of anticoagulant solution CPD-A[38] and maintained at 4C until processing.

Collection

Cells and tissues are usually collected under operating theatre conditions. An aseptic environment is fundamental to minimizing the risk of contamination. In either case, specific environmental conditions (container, temperature, transport solution, etc.) must be established to maintain cell viability and function according to cell bank requirements [40]. Umbilical cord blood is usually collected in a bag containing approximately 23 ml of anticoagulant solution CPD-A[38] and maintained at 4C until processing.

CHAPTER FIVE

Processing

Cell Selection

The presence of a high number of red blood cells in the sample is a problem because these cells can interfere with stem cell processing. Different methods are used to reduce or eliminate erythrocytes. For example, the hematocrit in umbilical cord blood can be reduced by adding hydroxyethyl starch, which induces erythrocyte aggregation and therefore facilitates sedimentation by gravity.

Two different automatic devices have been developed specifically for this purpose: Sepax and AXP. Sepax consists of a centrifuge and a pneumatic system with vacuum or pressure capability to fill or empty the separation chamber and lines, using sterile, The AXP AutoXpress platform is an automated fully closed system, specifically disposable processing kits with different configurations for dedicated protocols designed to reduce cord blood to a precise volume. This system has been developed with integrated sampling capability and a cryoprotectant line incorporating a sterile filter, potentially providing a truly closed system[41]. To eliminate residual erythrocytes entirely, for example from enzymatically digested adipose tissue, a specific lysis buffer (e.g. containing ammonium chloride) can be used. However, some authors have reported potential detrimental effects on stem cells with this treatment. Further cleaning of the cell suspension can be achieved using a sieve to retain residual extracellular matrix (e.g. fibres) or other tissue residues. In addition, with adequate pore size, this device can be used for cell selection purposes, as a function of cell size. Then, cells can be concentrated as a pellet in the bottom of a tube or a bag through centrifugation or stratification in layers.

Cell separation by centrifugal elutriation can be per-formed in a closed system with automated devices designed for this objective, resulting in improved cell yield and high reproducibility. For finer cell selection, microbeads with paramagnetic properties bearing antibodies against specific cell surface antigens can be used to capture cell populations based on their immunophenotype type. Positive selection uses antigens addressed against cells of interest[42] and negative selection uses antigens directed against cells that are not required [43]. In another immunology-based method, using fluorescent particles instead of paramagnetic beads, in combination with flow cytometry, a mixture of cells with different immune phenotypes can be sorted and each type of cell collected in a different container. This is called fluorescence-activated cell sorting (FACS) and is based on the specific light scattering and fluorescent characteristics of each cell.

Cryopreservation

Freezing is the method used most for successful long- term preservation of cells and tissues. To maintain cell viability, it is necessary to suspend cells in a cryoprotective solution and design freezing and thawing protocols. Dimethyl sulfoxide (DMSO) and glycerol are the products most often used as cryoprotectants [44]. DMSO is a cryoprotector widely used for stem cells derived from bone marrow, cord blood, dental pulp, placenta and adipose-derived adult stem cells[4].The presence of these substances lowers the freezing point, so that cell volume reduction during cooling is postponed to a lower temperature, and reduces the amount of ice crystals formed.[60].The main advantage of this apparatus is that it reaches a temperature close to that of nitrogen vapor. Cooling rates between 1 and 3C/min are suit able for a high number of human cell lineages Non-controlled freezing has been shown to be effective for HSCs from bone marrow[46] peripheral blood [47, 48,]and cord blood [49,50].

The freezing rate is a significant factor in viability assurance after storage and thawing. Controlled-rate freezers use accurate programs for cell freezing. The main advantage of this apparatus is that it reaches a temperature close to that of nitrogen vapor. Cooling rates between 1 and 3C/min are suitable for a high number of human cells lineages. The most common method to achieve freezing uses passive cooling devices, where the material is placed in a precooled polystyrene box or a precooled poly-carbonate container with ethanol or isopropanol at 80°C.

CHAPTER SIX

Umbilical Cord Blood Stem Cells

Cord-blood banking basically means collecting and storing the blood from within the umbilical cord (the part of the placenta that delivers nutrients to a foetus) after a baby is born. Cord blood contains blood-forming stem cells, which are potentially useful for treating diseases that require stem cell transplants (also called bone marrow transplants), such as certain kinds of leukemia or lymphoma, aplastic anemia, severe sickle cell disease, and severe combined immune deficiency. The value of cord blood stem cells over bone marrow.

Characteristics of Umbilical Cord

Umbilical cord blood (UCB) collected from the umbilical cord differs from the peripheral blood in its properties [51]. UCB can be cryopreserved and stored for >15 years with efficient recovery of stem cells on thawing [52].

Stem Cells Umbilical cord blood (UCB) collected from the umbilical cord differs from the peripheral blood in its properties [51]. DNA in these cells has a longer telomere length, which helps in long time hematopoiesis. It is a rich source of hematopoietic stem cells, which have the properties of self-renewal as well as the ability to differentiate into myeloid and lymphoid cell lineages [51].

Therapeutic Uses of Umbilical Cord Blood

Umbilical cord blood is cryopreserved for future use related to most medical conditions and disorders due to its lifesaving properties. It is also used for developing the therapies for incurable diseases. Some of the diseases cured are cancers and blood disorders which are considered to be fatal diseases. Umbilical cord blood solves many problems in the medical field as there are no counter effects after treatment. It also helps to recover from the harmful diseases which are not cured over generations as when these genetic disorders are cured then they do not pass on to next generation. Diseases such as Alzheimer's, Arthritis, Asthma, Cancer, Diabetes, Heart diseases and Strokes can be completely eradicated from a family history if cured using umbilical cord blood. It is a prevention method from the genetic disorder being passed down to the following generations. Like cord blood, the cord tissue which is termed as Wharton's jelly is found in the umbilical cord. This Wharton's jelly with Poly-Vinyl Alcohol is useful for mainly treating the skin wounds for humans. [53]

Advantages of Using Umbilical Stem Cells

As a source of haematopoietic stem cells for transplantation, there are several advantages of using umbilical cord blood stem cells over bone marrow stem cells, another major source of haematopoietic stem cells). An average of 120 mL of blood can be collected with no risk to either the mother or the baby [54]. The extraction of stem cells from the bone marrow also becomes increasingly difficult with aging as the red marrow space changes to a yellow-marrow as it becomes fat-filled with age. Umbilical cord blood stem cells also have the capability to be stored in a bank, allowing for their "off-the-shelf" use, unlike bone marrow [55].

RESEARCH AND POTENTIAL FUTURE USE OF UMBILICAL CORD BLOOD

There is increasing interest in the use of cord blood for novel indications in regenerative therapy or as a means of immune modulation. A recent systematic review identified a small number of published studies involving approximately 300 patients [56].

The most common emerging area described in these studies addressed the repair of neurological conditions, including cerebral palsy. A large study using umbilical cord blood in the treatment of cerebral palsy is ongoing. Indian Perspective India, being the second most populous country, possesses a great potential in the field of cord blood banking. Unfortunately, private cord blood banking has been projected as a form of 'biological insurance' and panacea for a long list of genetic and acquired illness. In India, there are four public blood banks and more than five private cord blood banks that are functional at present. Around 37% doctors and 42% laypersons erroneously felt that cord blood could be used to treat any genetic disorder including Duchenne muscular dystrophy and intellectual disability[57].

Cord blood transplants from related donors

HLA-identical sibling cord blood transplantation has been performed almost exclusively in children. The lower risk of both treatment-related mortality and chronic graft versus host disease makes cord blood transplantation a particularly successful option for children with haemoglobin opathies [58.]

Cord blood transplants in children from unrelated donors

Cord blood transplants from unrelated donors for children has been associated with sustained engraftment, a low incidence of graft versus host disease and no higher risk of leukaemic relapse [59].

Cord blood transplants in adults from unrelated donors

A study of the outcome of HSC transplants from unrelated donors in adults with acute leukaemia, published in 2004, is encouraging. [59]. Although the number of nucleated cells that were infused from cord blood in this study was significantly smaller when compared to bone marrow grafting, the incidence of chronic graft versus host disease, transplant-related mortality, relapse mortality and leukaemia-free survival were not significantly different between those receiving cord blood compared to adult donation of HSC [60].

Future possibilities in haematological disease

The cell dose of cord blood grafts remains of critical importance for speed of engraftment and survival after unrelated cord blood transplantation from unrelated donors, particularly in adults. a single, autologous unit is unlikely to be adequate for any individual over 50 kg. [61].

Cord Blood Transplantation

Person's defective stem cell is replaced by normal one. These normal stem cells could be isolated from bone marrow in the process of transplantation, peripheral blood and cord blood. The first autologous stem cell transplantation was undertaken. The transplantation was found to be successful without any graft versus host disease and still the patient is alive. The first successful umbilical cord blood stem cell transplant was reported as occurring in 1988 and his colleagues showed that the umbilical cord blood (UCB) contained sufficient HSCs for successful haematological reconstitution [62]are credited with performing the first successful unrelated umbilical cord blood transplant in the United States in 1994 [63].

Cord Blood Transplantation for Inherited Metabolic Disorders

Inherited metabolic disorders (IMD) are a heterogeneous group of genetic diseases. In most of these diseases, a single gene mutation causes an enzyme defect, which leads to the accumulation of substrates that are toxic and/ or interfere with normal cellular function. Many affected patients appear normal at birth. During infancy, however, they begin to exhibit disease manifestations, often including progressive neurological deterioration associated with absent or abnormal brain myelination. The ultimate result is death in later infancy or childhood. In the 1960s, Elizabeth Neufeld demonstrated that co-culture of fibroblasts from patients with two different IMDs (Hunter syndrome and Hurler syndrome) cross-corrected each other [64]; this established the basis for enzyme replacement therapy (ERT) and cellular therapy for that purpose.

ERT is available for selected IMDs and can be effective in ameliorating certain systemic disease manifestations, although there are limitations. ERT is unable to cross the blood brain barrier effectively and therefore does not alter the progression of neurologic symptoms [65,66]. Hematopoietic stem cell transplantation (HSCT) is indicated for a subset of IMDs including lysosomal storage diseases, peroxisomal storage diseases, and a few select others. The first HSCT for an IMD was performed in 1980 in a 1-year-old child with Hurler syndrome (mucopolysaccharidosis [MPS], type 1), a lysosomal storage disease, using bone marrow from his parents [67].

Among patients receiving CBT for Hurler syndrome, a shorter interval between diagnosis and CBT (<4.6 months [82%] versus >4.6 months [57%]) and a conditioning regimen containing busulfan and cyclophosphamide (75% versus 44% using other regimens) are associated with a significantly higher event-free survival [68].

Prognosis is strongly affected by the stage of the disease at the time of transplantation; children who undergo HSCT in pre-symptomatic or early disease stages fare better than those in symptomatic or advanced stages [69]. As such, HSCT is generally reserved for patients with pre-symptomatic or early disease. This is particularly challenging in the case of early infantile Krabbe disease. Symptoms typically become evident during the first 6 months of life, although there is evidence that damage occurs even prenatally. Krabbe disease is caused by mutations in the lysosomal enzyme galactosyl ceramidase, which then leads to an accumulation of psychosine followed by apoptosis of myelin-forming cells in the central and peripheral nervous systems. Affected babies develop irritability, spasticity, developmental regression, and seizures. Progression of symptoms is rapid and unrelenting, leading to death typically within 2 years. In 2005, the outcomes of 25 babies with Krabbe disease who received CBT were reported. The cohort included 11 presymptomatic new born (aged <1 month of life) along with 14 infants transplanted after the onset of symptoms [70].

Applications of cord blood banking

Beyond hematopoietic transplantation, additional potential applications of UCB include immunotherapy, tissue engineering and regenerative medicine. Work that was begun in the early 1980s revealed that cord blood was comparable to bone marrow in terms of its utility in stem cell transplantation [7]. In addition to its use as a substitute for bone marrow, cord blood has recently been used in a variety of regenerative medicine applications. Work done by different scientists has shown that cord blood contains a mixture of pluripotent stem cells capable of giving rise to cells derived from the endodermal, mesodermal, and ectodermal lineages[72].

Procedure of collecting stem cells storage in a stem cell bank

The Stem cell's capacity to repair and regenerate is the basis for all the researches in the field of stem cell therapy. This unique characteristic of stem cell is very attractive. The research and findings in this field of stem cell therapy proved to create a revolution in the field of medicine [73,74].

In recent investigation, the knowledge on stem cells and its role in treatment of different diseases developed awareness among people and moved them to adopt stem cell collection and preservation techniques. The stem cells are taken from the source from where the cells are harvested [75,76].Based on its source stem cells are classified as fetal stem cells, embryonic stem cells, umbilical cord stem cells and adult stem cells the cells formed from the zygotic division are called the embryonic stem cells because of its ability to develop into any type of cell [77,78]. The embryonic stem cells are removed from the embryos in vitro by adopting a technique called in vitro fertilization (IVF). In vitro fertilization is a method (used for treatment of sterile couples. In this method the sperm is inserted into the egg under controlled conditions in a laboratory condition[79,80]. The use of in vitro embryos for harvesting stem cells is a very accurate procedure which is done only by obtaining permission from the couple whose egg and sperm are used in developing the embryo. The harvested embryonic stem cells are developed through cell culture technique. [81,82]. The umbilical cord blood is a rich source of stem cells; it is a connection between the mother and baby through which nutrients are transferred from placenta to the baby in the womb. In order to collect the cord blood for stem cells, the cord between the placenta and the baby is clamped and a trained person collects the blood from the umbilical cord by using a needle [83,84]. The collected blood is transferred to the sample vial and sent for storage. Sterile conditions are maintained during the process of collection to avoid contamination of the sample. People with a family history of genetic disorders or diseases can preserve their baby's cord blood which can be used effectively in future treatment of various diseases [85,86].

The collected blood can be stored. The complete family can be benefited by storing umbilical cord stem cells. Adult stem cells are the existing cells in an adult. The cells of muscle tissue, bone marrow, skin cell and nerve cell are examples for adult stem cells [87,88].

CHAPTER SEVEN

Current Problems on Stem Cell Banking

In HSC (Higher Secondary Certificate) banking, the common problem is insufficient number of stem cells in each bankable unit of stem cells. The TNC (Transnational Corporation) of cord blood that are stored is on average less than the TNC values of samples recommended for transplantation[89]. Due to this limitation, many of the cord blood transfusions were initially performed on pediatric age group. In overcoming these issues, two units of cord blood - double Umbilical Cord Blood (dUCB) transplantation, was administered on adults, instead of one unit, to hasten the speed of short- and long-term engraftment. Even though the TNC was adequate, dUCB transplantation was associated with a slower engraftment time and higher rate of Non-Relapse Mortality (NRM) [60]. The other issues facing the stem cell therapeutic frontier are the emergence of alternative methods of treatment for diseases neurodegenerative diseases like Alzheimer's. William et al. in 2007 successfully induced neural cell formation from skeletal tissues with the application of neurodazine [90]. This is a cellular reprogramming technology, which can replace stem cell therapy. Other researchers also discovered that antidepressants are capable of stimulating stem cells in the brain to regenerate neurons and reduce amyloid peptides being laid down in hippocampus, indicating a possible cure treatment drug for Alzheimer's disease [91].

Storage of Stem Cells

There are many methods in storage of stem cells. These include cryopreservation, anhydrobiosis and lyophilization, which involved freezing, drying and freeze drying respectively[92]. Majority of stem cells are stored with cryopreservation method in stem cell banks. This method involves using low temperature to preserve the stem cells. These subzero temperature of -196ºC is generated by liquid nitrogen. There are two methods that are commonly used for storage. They are slow-cooling and rapid-cooling method. Currently, almost all stem cells are cryopreserved with the slow-cooling method with rapid thawing[93]. showed that rapid-cooling method for storage is found to be associated with higher recoverability of stem cells due to less intracellular injuries[94]. However, published that neither methods like cryopreservation nor freezing affect the quality of the HSCs under preservation [95].

Once the product has been successfully frozen, it has to be stored. Labelling must be adequate to maintain integrity and legibility during storage, identifying the product unequivocally and ensuring traceability. Long-term cryopreservation is critical for stem cell banking: the lower the temperature the longer the storage. The liquid nitrogen (196C) phase appears to be useful in achieving this aim. In addition, providing to an ultralow temperature, this liquid phase maintains a constant temperature, avoids undesirable oscillations and is easily monitored. The highly efficient recovery of functional hematopoietic progenitor and stem cells from cord blood cryopreserved for 15 years has been demonstrated [96]. To avoid the presence of liquid media that could be used as a vehicle for contaminating microorganisms, storage tanks based on the technology used in dry shipping have been developed. The dry shipper was designed for delivery of biological samples classified as non-hazardous at ultralow temperatures. The absorbent repels moisture and humidity but absorbs liquid nitrogen, allowing maintenance of a temperature in the range of the nitrogen vapour phase [97].

Selection of Cells for Transplantation and Delivery

The transplant program is fully dependent on the bank for the quality of stem cells. Stored stem cells can be used for autologous and allogeneic purposes. In the first case, selection is made mainly on the basis of cell quantity. In the second case, HLA matching is mandatory for some types of cells. The selection of HSCs for transplantation requires combining both cell dose and HLA matching. Possible HLA-matched cord blood units for patients are found from computerized registries [98]. Cell products can be shipped on long journeys in the frozen state, using dry shippers. Dry shippers allow the cells to remain frozen and can maintain temperatures below 150C for 14 days. Upon arrival, temperature is controlled. According to international standards, the temperature must be continuously controlled during transports.

CHAPTER EIGHT

Conclusions

Stem cell contributes to natural healing and plays an important role in regenerative medicine. Stem cell banking through long-term storage of different stem cells represents a basic source to store original features of stem cells for patient-specific clinical applications. Stem cells can heal the body, promote recovery, and offer an enormous amount of therapeutic potential. Cord blood holds promise for future medical procedures. Many scientists are still studying more ways to treat more diseases with cord blood. For example, many researchers are using patients' own cord blood in trials for cerebral palsy and Hypoxic ischemic encephalopathy. The increase in the use of these stem cells gave rise to the setting up of public and private facilities which could store the umbilical cord blood. As discussed in this paper, public banking facilities are favored over private alternatives. In addition, to ensure fair access to healthcare services to all, families at risk of specific diseases treatable by cord blood transplantation should have the opportunity to store their child's cord blood in a public registry for their exclusive use, as recommended by most of the policies surveyed. Cord blood banking has been available for more than 20 years, is well established and regulated, and has been involved in more than 30,000 stem cell transplants and thousands of regenerative therapies. Cord tissue banking has become available over the past 5–7 years as an adjunct to cord blood banking. The umbilical cord stem cells have been shown to be a promising step in the treatment of various illnesses. The increase in the usefulness of these stem cells gave rise to the setting up of public and private facilities which could store the umbilical cord blood.

CHAPTER NINE

References

1. Cryobanks/ Premier Cord Blood Bank, THE BIZZ 2010, Available at: URL: www. Cryobanksindia.

2. Life cell baby cord. Available at: URL: http://www.life cell international.com

3. Umbilical cord care (stump) information one Medicine Health.com. 2011 March 7. Available at: URL: http://www.emedicine health.com/ umbilical.

4. Ballen K. Challenges in umbilical cord blood stem cell banking for stem cell reviews and reports. Stem Cell Review. 2011;6(1).

5. Webb S. Banking on cord blood stem cells .Net Biotechnology. 2013; 31:585-8.

6. Gluckman E, Ruggeri A, Volt F, Cunha R. Milestones in umbilical cord blood transplantation. Br J Haematology. 2011;823-847

7. Waller-Wise R. Umbilical cord blood: information for childbirth educators. J Perinat Education.2011; 20(1):54–60.

8. McKenna D, Sheth J (2011). Umbilical cord blood: Current status & promise for the future. Indian Journal Medicine Research. 2011; 134:261–269.

9. Pace P, Blundell R. Stem Cells: Daddy or Chips—An Up to-Date Review on Ground-Breaking Discoveries in Stem Cell Research with Special Attention to iPSC Applications in Osteoarthritis. Stem Cell Discovery. 2016; 6: 39-44.

10. Bajada S, Mazakova I, Richardson JB, Asham makhi N. Updates on stem cells and their applications in regenerative medicine. Journal Tissue Engineering Regenerative Medicine.2008; 2: 169-183.

11. Diaferia GR, Cardano M, Cattaneo M, Spinelli C, Dessi S, Deblasio P. The science of stem cell biobanking: Investing in the future. Journal of

Cellular Physiology. 2011; 227:14-19.

12. Fratantoni JC, Hall CW, Neufeld EF. Hurler and Hunter syndromes: mutual correction of the defect in cultured fibroblasts. Science. 1968; 162(3853):570e2.

13. Vegvari A and Marko-Varga G. Clinical protein science and bio analytical mass spectrometry with an emphasis on lung cancer. Chem Rev. 2007; 110:3278-3298.

14. Sabel MS. Proteomics in melanoma biomarker discovery: great potential, many obstacles. International Journal Proteomics.2011.

15. Takahashi K, Tanabe k. Ohnuki M, Narita M. Induction of pluripotent stem cells from adult human fibroblasts by defined factors, Cell. 2007; 131 861-872.

16. Park IH, Zhao R, West JA, Yabuuchi A, Hongguang H., Reprogramming of human somatic cells to pluripotency with defined factors, Nature. 2008; 451 141-146

17. Conconi MT, Di Liddo R, Tommasini M, Calore C, Parnigotti PP. Phenotype and Differentiation Potential of Stromal Populations Obtained from Various Zones of Human Umbilical Cord: An Overview. The Open Tissue Engineering and Regenerative Medicine Journal. 2011; 4: 6-20

18. Bone Marrow Donors Worldwide Annual report, 2008.

19. Broxmeyer HE, Douglas GW, Hangoc G, Scott Cooper, Judith Bard. Human umbilical cord blood as a potential source of transplantable hematopoietic stem/progenitor cells. Proceedings of the National Academy Sciences USA.1989 ;86(10):3828-3832.

20. Kurtzberg J, Graham M, Casey J, Olson J, Stevens CE, Rubinstein P. The Use of Umbilical Cord Blood in Mismatched Related and Unrelated Hemopoietic Stem Cell Transplantation. Blood Cells. 1994; 20, 275-283

21. Wagner JE, Rosenthal J, Sweetman R, Xiao O, Stella MD. Successful transplantation of HLA-matched and HLA-mismatched umbilical cord blood from unrelated donors: analysis of engraftment and acute graft-versus-host disease. Blood. 1996;88(3):795-802

22. BBC NEWS. Cord blood stem cell transplant hopes lifted. Available at: URL:http://news.bbc.co.uk/2/hi/health/8462 488.stm. 2010.

23. Parikh Purvish M, Shah Pankaj M. Hematopoietic stem cells transplantation in India. Mediterr J Hematol Infect Dis. 2011; 3(1).

24. Di-Naro E, Ghezzi F, Raio L, Franchi M, D'Addario V. Umbilical cord morphology and pregnancy outcome. European Journal of Obstetrics &

Gynecology and Reproductive Biology. 2001; 96: 150-157.

25. Anna H, Lukasz P, Anna H. Characteristics of hematopoietic stem cells of umbilical cord blood. Cytotech. 2015; 67: 387-396.

26. Rubinstein P, Rosenfield RE., Adamson JW, Stevens C.E. Stored placental blood for unrelated bone marrow reconstitution. Blood.1993; 81, 1679–1690.

27. Conconi MT, Di Liddo R, Tommasini M, Calore C, Parnigotti PP. Phenotype and Differentiation Potential of Stromal Populations Obtained from Various Zones of Human Umbilical Cord: An Overview. The Open Tissue Engineering and Regenerative Medicine Journal. 2011; 4: 6-20.

28. LindenmairA, Hatanaka T, Koll wig G, Hennerbichler S, Gabriel C, Wolbank S, Redl H, Kasper C. Mesenchymal stem or stromal cells from amnion and umbilical cord tissue and their potential for clinical applications. Cells.2012; 1, 1061–1088.

29. Worgul BV, Smilenov L, Junk A, Zhou W. Atom heterozygous mice are more sensitive to radiation-induced cataracts than are their wild-type counterparts. Proceeding National Academy Sciences U.S.A. 2002; 99:9836–9839.

30. Secco M, Zucconi E, Vieira N.M, Fogaça LL, Cerqueira A, Carvalho MD, Jazedje T, Okamoto OK, Muotri AR, Zatz M. Multipotent stem cells from umbilical cord: Cord is richer than blood. Stem Cells. 2008; 26, 146–150.

31. Henry G, William PL, Bannister LH, Grey's Anatomy, 38th ed ; ELBS Churchill Livingstone: London, UK,1995.

32. Bongso A, Fong CY. The therapeutic potential, challenges and future clinical directions of stem cells from Wharton's jelly of the human umbilical cord. Stem Cell Reviews and Reports. 2013; 9, 226–240.

33. Tsagias N, Koliakos I, Karagiannis V, Eleftheriadou M, Koliakis GG. Isolation of mesenchymal stem cells using the total length of umbilical cord for transplantation purposes. Transfusion Medicine. 2011; 21(4), 253–261.

34. Dominici M, le Blanc K, Mueller I, Slaper-Cortenbach I, Marini F, Krause D, Deans R, Keating A, Prockop DJ, Horwitz E. Minimal criteria for defining multipotent mesenchymal stromal cells. The International Society for Cellular Therapy position statement. Cytotherapy. 2006; 8, 315–317.

35. Xue G, He M, Zhao J, Chen Y, Tian Y, Zhao B. Intravenous umbilical cord mesenchymal stem cell infusion for the treatment of combined

malnutrition nonunion of the humerus and radial nerve injury. Regenerative Medicine. 2011; 6, 733–741

36. Commission Directive 2003/94/EC, Official Journal of the European Union (2003) L262/22.

37. Ballen K, Broxmeyer HE, McCullough J. Current status of cord blood banking and transplantation in the United States and Europe, Biology. Blood Marrow Transplant. 2001; (7) 635.

38. Solves P, Perales A, Mirabet V. Optimizing donor selection in a cord blood bank, European Journal of Haematology. 2004; 72,107-112.

39. Zou S, Dodd RY, Stramer SL, Strong M. Probability of viremia with HBV, HCV, HIV and HTLV among tissue donors in the United States, New England Journal Medicine.2004; 351, 751-759

40. Larrea L, de la Rubia J, Soler MA. Quality control of bacterial contamination in autologous peripheral blood stem cells for transplantation, Haematological. 2004; 89, 1232-1237.

41. Armitage S. cord blood processing: volume reduction, Cell Preservation Technology.2006; 4 ,9-16

42. Carr T, Evans P, Campbell S, Bass P, Albano J. Culture of human renal tubular cells: positive selection of kallikrein containing cells, Immunopharmacology. 1999; 44. 161-167.

43. Sabel MS. Proteomics in melanoma biomarker discovery: great potential, many obstacles. International Journal Proteomics.2011

44. Polge C, Smith AU, Parkes AS, Revival of spermatozoa after vitrification and dehydration at low temperatures, Nature. 164. 666.

45. Thirumala S, Scott Goebel W, Woods EJ. Clinical grade adult stem cell banking, Organogenesis. 2009; 5, 143-154

46. Clark J, Pati A, D. McCarthy. Successful cryopreservation of human bone marrow does not require a controlled rate freezer, Bone Marrow Transplant.1991; 7 .121-125.

47. Kawano Y, Lee CL, Watanabe T. Cryopreservation of mobilized blood stem cells at a higher cell concentration without the use of a programmed freezer, Annals Hematology.2004; 83, 50-54.

48. Perez Oteyza J, Bornstein R, Corral M, et al., Controlled rate versus uncontrolled rate cryopreservation of peripheral blood versus uncontrolled rate cryopreservation of peripheral blood progenitor cells: a prospective multicenter study. Group for Cryobiology and Biology of Bone Marrow Transplantation (CBTMO), Spain Haematological.1998; 83. 1001-1005.

49. Solves P, Larrea L, Soler MA, Mirabet V, Carbonell F, Franco FM. Programmed versus non-programmed freezing of umbilical cord blood, Haematologica.2000; 85 ,890-891.

50. Itoh T, Minehishi M, Fushimi J. A simple controlled rate freezing method without a rate controlled programmed freezer provides optimal conditions for both large scale and small-scale cryopreservation of umbilical cord blood cells, Transfusion. 2003; 43, 1303-1308.

51. Verma V, Tabassum N, Yadav CB, Kumar M, Singh AK, Singh MP. Cord blood banking: An Indian perspective. Cell Molecular Biology.2016; 62:1

52. Ballen KK, Gluckman E, Broxmeyer HE. Umbilical cord blood transplantation: the first 25 years and beyond. Blood. 2013; 122:491-8.

53. Cassar P. and Blundell R. The Use of Umbilical Stem Cells. Open Journal of Pathology. 2016; 6, 41-56. https://doi.org/10.4236/ojpathology.2016.61007

54. Rogers, I. and Casper, RF. Umbilical Cord Blood Stem Cells. Best Practice & Research; Clinical Obstetrics & Gynaecology.2004; 18, 893-908. https://doi.org/10.1016/j.bpobgyn.06.004

55. Weiss ML. and Troyer DL. Stem Cells in the Umbilical Cord. Stem Cell Reviews and Reports. 2006; 2, 155-162. https://doi.org/10.1007/s12015-006-0022-

56. Iafolla MAJ, Tay J, Allan DS. Transplantation of umbilical cord blood-derived cells for novel indications in regenerative or immunomodulatory therapy: a scoping review of clinical studies. Biology Blood Marrow Transplant; 2014; 20:20–577.

57. Tuteja M, Agarwal M, Phadke SR. Knowledge of cord blood banking in general population and doctors: A questionnair based survey. Indian Journal Pediatrics.2016; 83: 238-41

58. Gluckman E, Rocha V, Boyer-Chammard A, Locatelli F, Arcese W, Pasquini R. Outcome of cordblood transplantation from related and unrelated donors. Eurocord Transplant Group and the European Blood and Marrow Transplantation Group. New England Journal Medicine. 1997; 337:373–38.

59. Rocha V, Labopin M, Sanz G, Arcese W, Schwerdtfeger R, Bosi A, Jacobsen N, Ruutu T, Frassoni F. Acute Leukemia Working Party of European Blood and Marrow Transplant Group; Eurocord-Netcord Registry. Transplants of umbilical cord blood or bone marrow from unrelated donors in adults with acute leukemia. New England Journal Medicine.2004; 351:2276–8514.

60. Bornstein R, Flores AI, Montaban MA, del Rey MJ, de la Serna J, Gillian F. A modified cord blood collection method achieves sufficient cell levels for transplantation in most adult patients. Stem Cells. 2005; 23:324–34.

61. Rachael E Hough, Ajay J Vora, John E Wagner. Innovative strategies to improve outcome of unrelated donor umbilical cord blood transplantation. Bloodmed [www.bloodmed.com/400000/default.asp].2005.

62. Watt SM, Contreras M. Stem Cell Medicine: Umbilical Cord Blood and Its Stem Cell Potential. Seminars in Fetal and Neonatal Medicine. 2005; 2 10: 209-220. 29

63. Kurtzberg J, Graham M, Casey J, Olson J, Stevens, CE. and Rubinstein P. The Use of Umbilical Cord Blood in Mismatched Related and Unrelated Hemopoietic Stem Cell Transplantation. Blood Cells. 1994; 20, 275-283

64. Fratantoni JC, Hall CW. Neufeld EF. Hurler and Hunter syndromes: mutual correction of the defect in cultured fibroblasts. Science. 1968; 162(3853):570e2.

65. Tokic V, Barisic I, Huzjak N, Petkovic G, Fumic K, Paschke E. Enzyme replacement therapy in two patients with an advanced severe (Hurler) phenotype of mucopolysaccharidosis I. European Journal Pediatrics.2007; 166(7):727-32.

66. Shull RM, Kakkis ED, McEntee MF, Kania SA, Jonas AJ, Neufeld EF. Enzyme replacement in a canine model of Hurler syndrome. Proceedings Natlional Academy Sciences USA. 1994;91(26):12937-41.

67. Hobbs JR, Hugh-Jones K, Barrett AJ, Byrom N, Henry K, James DC, Lucas CF Reversal of clinical features of Hurler's disease and biochemical improvement after treatment by bone-marrow transplantation. Lancet. 1981; 2(8249):709-12.

68. Boelens JJ, Rocha V, Aldenhoven M. Risk factor analysis of outcomes after unrelated cord blood transplantation in patients with hurler syndrome. Biology Blood Marrow Transplant. 2009; 15(5):618-625

69. Tracy E, Aldrink J, Panosian J. Isolation of oligodendrocyte-like cells from human umbilical cord blood. Cytotherapy 2008; 10(5):518-525.

70. Escolar ML, Poe MD, Provenzale JM, Richards KC, Wall D, Wood S. Transplantation of umbilical-cord blood in babies with infantile Krabbe's disease. New England Journal Medicine .2005; 352(20):2069-2081

71. McKenna D, Sheth J. Umbilical cord blood: Current status & promise for the future. Indian Journal Medicine Reserch. 2011; 134:261–269.

72. Gluckman E, Ruggeri A, Volt F, Cunha R, Boudiedir K. Milestones in umbilical cord blood transplantation. British Journal Haematology. 2011; 154(4):441–447

73. Kaye J. Ethical implications of the use of whole genome methods in medical research. European Journal Human Genetics.2010; 18:398-403.

74. Kegley JA. Challenges to informed consent. EMBO Reports. 2004; 5:832-836.

75. Howard HC, Joly Y, Avard D, Laplante N. Informed consent in the context of pharmacogenomic research: ethical considerations. Pharmacogenomics Journal. 2011; ,1:155-161.

76. Behrman RE. Letter from AMP to the Secretary's Advisory Committee on Genetics, Health, and Society.2007.

77. Jensen JS. Arterial hypertension, micro albuminuria and risk of ischemic heart disease. Hypertension. 2000; 35:898-903

78. Shimizu T and Nakagawa K. Novel Drug Development of the Next-Generation T790M Mutant Specific Epidermal Growth Factor Receptor Tyrosine Kinase Inhibitors for the Treatment of Advanced Non-Small Cell Lung Cancer. Biochem Anal Biochem. 2016; 5:258

79. Orlic D, Kajstura J, Chimenti S, Jakoniuk I, Pickel J. Bone marrow cells regenerate infarcted myocardium. Nature.2001; 410:701-705

80. Klahr S, Gerald J Beck, Hunsicker L. The effects of dietary protein restriction and blood-pressure control on the progression of chronic renal disease. Modification of Diet in Renal Disease Study Group. New England Journal Medicine.1994; 330:877-884.

81. Turnbull F, et al. Effects of different blood pressure-lowering regimens on major cardiovascular events in individuals with and without diabetes mellitus: results of prospectively designed overviews of randomized trials. Arch Intern Med. 2005; 165:1410-1419.

82. Strauer BE, Brehm M, Zeus T, Kostering M. Repair of infarcted myocardium by autologous intracoronary mononuclear bone marrow cell transplantation in humans. National Medicine. 2001; 7: 430-436.

83. Wazer DE. Loss of p53 protein during radiation transformation of primary human mammary epithelial cells. Molecular Cell Biology. 1994; 14:2468–2478.

84. Wolff S. Aspects of the adaptive response to very low doses of radiation and other agents. Mutation Research. 1996; 358:135–142

85. Worgul BV, Smilenov L, Junk A, Zhou W. Atom heterozygous mice are more sensitive to radiation-induced cataracts than are their wild-

type counterparts. Proceeding National Academy Sciences U.S.A.2002; 99:9836–9839.

86. Takeoka Y. IN-situ preparation of poly (L-lactic acid-co-glycolic acid)/hydroxyapatite composites as artificial bone materials. Polymer Journal. 2015; 47:164-170.

87. Albertsson AC and Varma KI. Recent Developments in Ring Opening Polymerization of Lactones for Biomedical Applications. Biomacromolecules.2003; 4:1466-1686.

88. Chang HK. Clinical characteristics and management of benign transient non-organic ileus of neonates: A single centre experience. Yonsei Medicine Journal. 2014; 55:157-161.

89. Keersmaekers CL, Mason BA, Keersmaekers J, Ponzini M, Mlynarek R. Factors affecting umbilical cord blood stem cell suitability for transplantation in an in-utero collection program. Transfusion: Epub ahead of print; doi: 2013; 10.1111/trf.12340 Available from: http://www.ncbi.nlm.nih.gov/pubmed/23869580

90. Williams DR, Lee MR, Song YA, Ko SK, Kim GH, Shin I. Synthetic Small Molecules that Induce Neurogenesis in Skeletal Muscle. Journal Am Chem Social. 2007; 129:9258–9259.

91. Kim HJ, Kim W, Kong SY. Antidepressants for neuro-regeneration: from depression to Alzheimer's disease. Archives Pharmacal Reseach.2013; 36(11):1279–1290.

92. Devireddy R, Thirumala S. Preservation protocols for human adipose tissue-derived adult stem cells. Methods Mol Biology. 20111; 702:369-394.

93. Diaferia GR, Cardano M, Cattaneo M, Spinelli C, Dessi S, Deblasio P. The science of stem cell biobanking: Investing in the future. Journal of Cellular Physiology. 2011; 227:14-19

94. Djuwantono T, Wirakusumah FF, Achmad TH, Sandra F, Halim D, Faried A. A comparison of cryopreservation methods: Slow cooling vs. rapid-cooling based on cell viability, oxidative stress, apoptosis, and CD34+ enumeration of human umbilical cord blood mononucleated cells. BMC Research Notes.2011; 4(371):1-9.

95. Antoniewicz-papis J, Lachert E, Wozniak J, Janik K, Letowska M (2013). Methods of freezing cord blood hematopoietic stem cells. Transfusion. Epub ahead of print. Available from:2013; http://www.ncbi.nlm.nih.gov/pubmed/23621822

96. Ballen KK, Gluckman E, Broxmeyer HE. Umbilical cord blood transplantation: the first 25 years and beyond. Blood.2013; 122:491-8.
97. Wall DA. Selection of cord blood units for transplantation, Bone Marrow Transplant. 2008; 42, 1-7.